DARE TO BELIEVE

MIRACLES IN OUR EVERYDAY WORLD

PHYLLIS A. WILLOUGHBY

To Tonya,

Thank you for your support! I watched you develop into an Amazing Realtor! Keep up the great work. May God continue to Bless you!

Grateful,
Phyllis A. Willoughby

DARE TO BELIEVE
MIRACLES IN OUR EVERYDAY WORLD
Copyright © 2023 Phyllis A. Willoughby
All rights reserved.

No portion of this publication may be reproduced, stored in any electronic system, or transmitted in any form or by any means without the written permission from the author. Brief quotations may be used in literary reviews.

All stories included in this publication were written and used with permission from the contributors.

ISBN-13: 979-8-9874187-1-0

DEDICATION

I dedicate this book:

To my mother – Rev. Delores C. Willoughby, who now is ambulatory and non-verbal. However, my mother was my biggest cheerleader! She instilled in me "Never Give Up". She always wanted to write book about my paternal Grandfather who was also a believer and always lived below means. Although, this book is not about him but I know my mother will be just as proud to read about "Our Father".

To my loving Husband – Elton I. Cook. Thank you for your love and support for the last 18 years. I also appreciate you for allowing me the space and quiet time to write this book. Thank you, Honey, "I Love You."

To my dad, Norman W. Willoughby
Who taught me when you pray, you must have Faith in God and leave it there for Him to answer your prayers.

To my son, Alexander W. Hines
My heartbeat, you are smart, intelligent, courageous and funny. Hold on to God's unchanging hands and He will guide you through this complicated life.

To Alex Then – My Life Coach #1
Alex you have been coaching me since 2008….you helped me simplify this complicated life. You started me on this

journey of writing this book 10 years ago. Thank you, Alex for being one of God's Angels here on Earth! Most of all for being obedient to God! You came to my rescue and helped me get out of my wheelchair for good. Praise God! On May 4, 2023, God said "your work is done here, my good and faithful servant." Rest in Heaven, my Friend.

To Ken Altenbach – My Life Coach #2
Thank you, Ken for identifying that it was my soul yearning to complete my book and you helped me to stay on course.

To Dr. Sheila Y. Garris – Better known as "Dr. Feel Good."
Dr. Sheila Y. Garris was a friend who called me every single morning while I was in the hospital and she would say "Good Morning Sunshine"….it meant so much to me. I could see the sunshine even when it was raining. "Dr. Feel Good" always made people feel better. On, Dec 7, 2022, Wednesday morning my friend did not wake up! Rest in Heaven my friend.

To Marian Foxworth – A long-time Friend
Marian was a friend who always encouraged me through all my ups and downs. She was my most consistent friend for over forty years without any interruptions. On Oct 8, 2022, Saturday morning she did not wake up! Rest in Heaven my friend.

To John P. Yancey – My business partner, client and friend. Thank you, Mr. Yancey for having the confidence in me and allowing me to be your trusted advisor on numerous projects. Rest in Heaven, my friend.

ACKNOWLEDGEMENTS

I would like to acknowledge all those that shared their stories and contributed to this book. Thank you for sharing your miracles.

Ken Longo: The Miracle Wedding
Leslie Wills: Leslie's Story
Leila Holt: Leila's Testimony
Glenda C. Powell: Glenda's Miracles and More Miracles
Darren Kerr: I Asked for a Little Bird
John P. Yancey: Short Story
Chad Ingram: Chad's Story
Philex Rodriguez: Philex's Story

Phyllis Willoughby

INTRODUCTION
The Three Treasures

I have three treasures that I discovered. First was a letter I received from my group of spiritual guides.

Dear friend,

The journey you are taking is indeed special and important for your message for the world. To believe in oneself and to follow ones intuition is important.

We are with you. Let us help you and more importantly believe that we are with you and all will be well.
Trust. Trust. Trust.

Your group of guides

I did not remember receiving this letter when I read it— it was like reading it for the first time— I could feel the energy exuding from the letter. This was confirmation it was time to finish my book. The second treasure was a yellow, unaddressed card. I opened it; it was a Christmas card. I thought it was blank. I opened it and read the message that was written for me from God. When I read it—I couldn't believe it!— I knew right then without a shadow of a doubt it was time for me to step up and do what God has asked me to do!

Phyllis,

Your Lord. My child. Blessed you be. May you find truth in Me. For I am there for you always. The test you experience are my teachings, My love, My guidance for you. Do not fear for I am with you always. You have a gift I have bestowed. You will see and know it and watch it grow. Keep your Faith for tests are sure to grow. Don't worry my child for I am home. Look inside and see my plan for you. Stop the fretting and the fear. I have shown you my love, my gifts, my strength, as you wished. Now hold on to those as I grant your wish. My dear, your life could be full of Bliss. Take a bow. Feel the crowd.

My child, I've already granted your wish!

With Love,
Glenda

The third treasure was a homemade anniversary card from my son Alex in 2014. It was his first year in college. The card was truly heartfelt and entertaining.

DARE TO BELIEVE: Miracles in our Everyday World

After reading these three treasures, I had confirmation of what my mission was, to complete God's Book.

I am clear this book is not about me. Yes, I have shared some stories, but it is the lesson or message in the story that can help one person get through to the other side of their storm. My mom would always say, "This too shall pass". Guess what? It does. You have to stand in faith and know that God is with you in every moment. He will carry you through; just let Him! God wants you to know how powerful He really is,. Just accept Him as your Lord and Savior, and He will make your crooked road map straight. To God be the Glory!

As I am writing this book I am listening intently to God's Voice and feeling His Energy as conduit to relay His Message to the world. God is using me to share some personal stories about myself that I thought I would be embarrassed to share. However, God reminded me it is not about me. It is about helping others to see and feel some light in their lives. If that means sharing some uncomfortable information, then it is for the greater good.

Let the God in us shine through like a ray of sunshine and bring light to this dark world.

Feel God's Energy: it leads, guides, protects, and conquers. Just know that God is with us All the Time! He never leaves us; all we have to do is call on him! All God wants is for us to lean on Him and not our own understanding. God sees all and knows all.

Consider something as small as the time I lost my rings and I asked God to show me where they were. After passively looking for four days, I stopped and asked God to just show me...guess what? He did! He took me directly to a pair of jean shorts left pocket....and there they were! I said, "Thank you God! You see and know all."

Phyllis Willoughby

TABLE OF CONTENTS

DEDICATION iii
ACKNOWLEDGEMENTS v
INTRODUCTION vii
TABLE OF CONTENTS xiii
MY STORY 1
A MOTHER'S LOVE 11
MY MOTHER'S MIRACULOUS JOURNEY 13
THE 72-HOUR MIRACLE 19
MIRACLES HAPPEN EVERY DAY, EVERYWHERE, TO EVERYONE 21
MIRACLES WE TAKE FOR GRANTED 39
GOD'S MESSAGE TO THE WORLD 41
I ASKED FOR A LITTLE BIRD 47
MORE MIRACLES 51
DARE TO BELIEVE 61
30 DAYS OF JOURNALING 63
ABOUT THE AUTHOR 95

MY STORY

I am Almighty God. This book is a guide for believers to know their faith, how faith works, and miracles happen every day and everywhere.
Believe in Me.

I will guide your path. You must know I am with you always. Listen and hear Me speak to you. I am a healer, a protector, provider, and way-maker. I will provide all your needs.
This book will show you how anyone can and will be blessed. Just believe in Me.

How you will be blessed is up to you. Just call on Me and I will be there! I am using Phyllis as an instrument to share my goodness and understand the meaning of faith. You will read stories that speak to you.

On January 25, 2012, I had an adverse reaction to medication. That day I felt like my life had stopped. I felt listless but still took my meds on time. My housekeeper at the time had been there for about two hours. She asked me if I needed her to take me to the hospital. I said, "No, I will be okay. I just needed a power nap." Two hours later, I got up and took a shower before heading to my corporate office to print and fax some time sensitive documents. I decided to work out of the Resource Center (Thank God) A Miracle, I never worked at this location. I usually worked in a secluded corner of the building, but this day I didn't. I was faxing documents, and I was feeling so weak. One of the employees walked in and I said to her ,"I'm not feeling well if anything happens." She immediately told her boss, Queenie. She came to me and asked if I was okay and if I needed water. I remember thinking, 'Maybe water would help.' She brought me water and said, as she went back to her office, if I need anything else, please let her know. By this time, I was sitting down trying to complete and fax a home inspection addendum to my client. I drank the water and told myself I was feeling better until I realized something was going on. I called my friend Dr. Sheila Y. Garris (a diabetic and hypertension specialist) and asked her what were the symptoms for low blood sugar? She told me just come over and she would test me. She just had emergency eye surgery that week. I told her I could not drive to her. She said to get someone from the office to bring me there, which was approximately seven miles away. I tried to gather my belongings; I could not use my hands to pick up my paperwork. That is when I yelled out for help! Queenie came in. I asked her to take me to the Patient First (a local clinic); they were right up the street and the ones that had prescribed the medication that I reacted to.

Thank God. Queenie dropped everything to take me to Patient First. I was so weak I could barely walk. She got her co-worker to help me get in her truck.

Once we got to Patient First, Queenie went inside to get a wheelchair. While I was waiting, I felt this stretching feeling on the right side of my head. Queenie and a technician came out of the clinic to bring me in, as they were registering me, I passed out. When I woke up, there were a lot of people poking and prodding me. First, they thought I was having a stroke until they were able to test and realize it wasn't. Then they thought I was having a reaction to the medication they had prescribed. They called the ambulance to take me to Sentara Leigh Hospital.

I didn't know what was happening to me. I asked myself, "Am I dying"? I just started praying. By the time I got to the hospital, I was so weak I didn't have use of my arms or my legs. The doctor started ordering a battery of tests. I continued praying and suddenly I felt God's Presence and heard His voice say, "It is only temporary…it is the test for the testimony." Immediately I felt this sense of peace beyond my own understanding— A Miracle —I displayed no fear because God spoke to me, and I believed it to be true. This is how faith works. In the midst of my healing, God was able to reach others through me who also needed healing. The doctors still did not understand what was going on, but I quickly learned it was not for them to understand. It was God's Time to shine through me. God was working through me to show what the power of prayer can do and will do! God allowed so many people to witness my Miracle. After weeks in the hospital, I was discharged in a wheelchair to receive physical and occupational therapy at home.

On the morning of February 11, 2012, my mother called me to tell me she had a dream I would be walking soon. We both praised God with excitement! I claimed it and received it! To God be the Glory!

Later that night I received an unexpected visitor, to my surprise it was my life coach, Alex. He had other plans that evening and was diverted to my house by God. I was in bed at the time, and my husband put me in a wheelchair and rolled me into my family room to greet my surprise visitor. He saw the shock in my face to see him, especially at that time of night. He told me he hadn't planned on coming, but God told him he was needed here. I said, "Thank you." First, he asked if he could pray with me, and of course I said yes! He proceeded to pray. While praying he grabbed my hands and lifted me out of the wheelchair to stand. I suddenly felt this overwhelming energy racing up and down my legs. He said, "Trust me," as he guided me step-by-step, walking around my family room, holding his hands. He then called out to my husband to bring the walker to us. My husband was in shock to see me standing. He handed the walker to my coach. Alex put my hands on the walker and proceeded to guide me throughout my house. He listened to God and showed up and showed out! I never sat back in that wheelchair again! A Miracle took place that night!

To God be the Glory!

What is a Miracle?

A Miracle is a surprising and welcome event that is not explainable by natural or scientific laws and is therefore considered to be the work of divine agency. Or a miracle can be described as a highly improbable or extraordinary event, development or accomplishment that brings welcome consequences. A Miracle is the outcome of a positive mindset.

You have to have faith!

Faith dictates your life and your footsteps that follow! Know who and whose you are! Faith orders your steps.

I remember waking up one morning in excruciating pain. I could barely get out of bed to go to the bathroom. A friend just happened to call, and I told her what I was experiencing, and she said she would be right over. I knew then that I needed to get up and unlock the door for her. It took me literally ten minutes to get to the door to unlock it. The pain was so bad I could only inch walk to the door. I finally inched back to my bed. I was trying to get up to go to the bathroom just as the doorbell rang; my feet would not move anymore. As my friend entered my bedroom, she saw me standing urinating on myself because I could not move another step. She was a blessing. She cleaned me up first then she cleaned my carpet so it would not stain. Afterwards, she took me to the chiropractor I was referred to. It took three people to get me on and off the table, she tried different instruments and nothing could touch that area. The doctor said since she was unsuccessful it would be no charge. My friend took me home and made me some soup since I had not eaten that day. Then I suddenly remembered I had a session with Coach Alex. She said to me, "Cancel the appointment." I told her, "He is supposed to be a healer as well, so let's try anyway." She took me to his home.

I walked into Alex's home on two canes, screaming with every step from sciatic nerve pain. I was so embarrassed, his two daughters were there looking at me. Two hours later, I walked out with only one cane for stability, something that the chiropractor could not do.

I remember thinking, 'How did that happen?'

He never touched me. My friend and Alex's daughters became witnesses that day!

I realized God's Miracle. God gives people gifts and talents to help us in our daily lives!

Believe.

There are human angels on Earth; are you one of them?

Feel God's Energy and hear His Voice speaking to you!

If you allow God to direct your path you will receive bountiful blessings (miracles) in your life.

God wanted me to share that we are all blessed with miracles everyday of our lives; they are just in different sizes. We are all walking and talking miracles, every day. People take for granted that when we wake up in the morning, we believe it was them that woke them up. In fact, God chooses to wake you up! That's A Miracle. My friend Dr. Sheila Y. Garris did not wake up on December 22, 2022. Rest in Peace My Friend.

I was headed to a colleague's funeral. Just as I got to the church, I realized I needed to park across the street. I just reacted and turned left into an oncoming truck. We both looked at each other in fear because we were about to collide. Suddenly, I felt God's Presence, and He pushed my truck enough to miss colliding. I was in shock along with those who had witnessed God's Miracle in the flesh.

Open your eyes and see all the miracles in your life and share them.

Thank You, God for allowing me to be a vessel for You to share Your Message. Wake up, everyone! Don't be sleepwalking in this world. Add some light on a daily basis through word or deed to this dark world that we are living in now. Motivate and inspire others to be their best selves. How can I be impactful by being obedient to God and planting seeds of goodness?

P-power up
R-release negativity
A-Acknowledge God
Y-Yourself and others

Follow me and you will ease your path to victory!

Walking in the spirit of God. Feel his spirit and make a difference and feel the joy.

Let your light shine through the darkness of this world.

Be a blessing and watch how God blesses you!

Just think, if only 50% of the world would have the same attitude "to be a blessing" how that would change the dynamics of the world. It would remove so much hate! That would be A Miracle!! So, I challenge everyone to be a blessing on a daily basis and be part of someone else's miracle. You will become the MIRACLE.

I am Great. I am all-knowing and caring God.
I'm always here for you and you don't need an appointment to reach me.

When you believe in Me, you will experience blessings and miracles in your life.

Gratitude is the gateway to abundance.

Phyllis Willoughby

A MOTHER'S LOVE

A mother's love: what we do for our children. My son is a rapper and was doing his second tour in Japan. He called me from the airport, and he asked me to pray with him and his friend for safe travels. Of course, I did. The next morning, I felt this emptiness. I sent him a text with no response. I prayed he was okay, but I still felt this uneasiness in my gut. I remember asking my dad if he had spoken to him. He said, "No, but your nephew has." So, I called my nephew, and he said he spoke to him a couple days ago. I didn't have any of his band members' numbers. My nephew went on social media only to find out his band members had posted "FREE XELA!". A mother's true nightmare. My son was in jail in another country for possession of a small amount of weed. The amount really didn't matter. It was illegal in that country along with his prescription meds. I was devastated. I cried. I reached out to whoever I could to get some answers. I was finally able to reach the US Embassy, and they confirmed he was incarcerated. He was not allowed a phone call.

For months I literally felt what he was going through. When he had an asthma attack, I felt it. I confirmed with the embassy they had to take him to the hospital to be treated.

On another occasion, I was driving to Eastern Shore, Maryland for dinner with my parents when I pulled into the parking lot. I started throwing up, I felt like someone was kicking me in the back. I reached out to the US Embassy again, and they informed me he had food poisoning and had been in an altercation. That's when I asked God to release him from me. Thank You, God! From that day God protected me from feeling what he was going through.

Fast forward five months, he was facing fifteen years of hard labor and a $30,000 fine. He was found guilty, but God stepped in! He was rearrested by immigration for overextending his VISA. That's when he finally got to place his phone call. I heard his voice for the first time in months. I just cried and praised God; he was finally coming home. No jail time and no fine, he just can't go to Japan for five years. He was immediately deported home. LOOK AT GOD! A MIRACLE !

God says believe in Me; I am the way. I will make a way out of no way!

MY MOTHER'S MIRACULOUS JOURNEY

In February 2016, my mother had major back surgery at Chesapeake Regional Medical Center. One week later, she was discharged to Lake Taylor Rehab Center with no management for the excruciating pain that she was experiencing.

I remember watching her in pain, and it would make my teeth cringe. I said to the nurse something needed to be done to relieve her pain. The following week I was with her, and a CNA came in to change her. She said, "No," turned to me and said, "You do it,". I said, "Okay, mom but I need you to help." As changed her, I had my back toward her, I felt her shaking, then her leg dropped. I turned and looked at her, and asked, "Are you okay?" She had a blank stare and wasn't speaking. I asked her, "Do you want me to call the nurse?" No response. I grabbed her hand and asked her to squeeze mine. She didn't. That's when I called the nurse in. The nurse checked her and said, "I think it is the effects of the medication she is taking." She was wrong. My mother was having a major stroke. When my dad came in, I told him what had taken place, we noticed her lip was hanging and my dad kept asking her to close her mouth.

The next day my mother was rushed to Sentarta Leigh Emergency room because her eyes were racing, like running after each other. I have never seen anything like that in my life. I was sure my mother had a massive stroke that had damaged her frontal lobe. After weeks in the hospital, my mother was discharged to Harbor's Edge Assisted Living with a feeding tube and an open wound.

I informed the nurses of the open wound on my mother's tailbone and they had to be very careful when changing her so her wound would not get infected. Guess what?

It got infected! I was watching the CNAs change her, and I saw fluid gushing out of the wound. I immediately contacted her surgeon. I told him what was going on with my mother's wound. He explained to me that if they didn't get the infection under control that he would have to go back in to clean the infection out.

The next day my mother was rushed to Sentara Norfolk General Hospital because the infection had gone to her brain. The doctors there did not want to go behind another surgeon, so she was transferred back to Chesapeake Regional Medical Center, where the original surgeon could clean out her wound. Thank, God the surgery was a success! The following day, she seemed to be doing well, until I came in to sit with her. She felt warm to me. I asked the nurse to take her temperature. She told me they had already taken it and it, was fine. I said, "Humor me, please." She took her temperature and it read 102 degrees. I asked what could be done to bring down the temperature? The on-call doctor was called to order Tylenol.

One hour passed, no Tylenol. Then I noticed my mother seemed listless. I called the nurse in again, this time to take my mother's blood pressure, which was not due to be taken again for another two hours. She reluctantly took her pressure and discovered her blood pressure was very low. Again, I asked what we can do? Again, she referred to the doctor on call.

Another hour passed. My mother seemed to be slipping away before my eyes! To God be the Glory!

I called her surgeon's home number and cell back-to-back. He realized it had to be an emergency since it was after 10 p.m. and I was calling both numbers. He called me back, and I explained to him that the on-call doctor was not responding, it had been over two hours, and my mother appeared to be slipping away. Within thirty minutes my mother was receiving a blood transfusion and Tylenol.

It was at that moment I realized I couldn't be angry with my sister for being late to keep our mother company, it was A Miracle . God used me to save my mother's life. The on-call doctor never responded, and my sister did not have her surgeon's personal numbers. Before I left my mother, she had received two bags of blood and her temperature started coming down. I said, "Thank You, God. A Miracle. Had my sister been on time, my mother would not be here.

My mother was discharged back to Lake Taylor Rehab Center's hospital floor. I learned that when you have a loved one in the hospital, you need someone there 24/7 to advocate for them. My mother had four advocates sitting with her. I came in at 3:00 p.m. one day and her chart was signed off that she had been turned over every 2 hours from 7:00 a.m. to 7:00 p.m.

My mother was finally discharged to Kempsville Health and Rehab Center. Everything was fine until the CNA came in to take her vitals. Her temperature was back up and blood pressure was down and dropping. I called the nurse to call the doctor. After thirty minutes I made the executive decision to call 911 to take her to the hospital. In spite of the nurse telling me that I would be responsible for the cost of the ambulance. The EMT was getting the release papers signed by the nurse and found out that the doctor still had not responded. She then made the decision to not charge me. A Miracle .

The hospital discovered that my mother had developed an infection. She was treated and discharged back to the rehab center. After a month, my mother was discharged home to hospice. The doctors had given her six months to live.; I decided not to share that part with the family, we are a family of believers. My mother is an ordained minister, and we know God is a healer.

My mother came home with a feeding tube which caused her to develop diabetes. We had to give her insulin, along with other meds. We were taking turns with shifts to care for my mother, even at home. I remember praying just to see her eyes open. Seven months later I discovered "binaural beats". When I decided to search for healing of the brain "binaural beats", I found one that said, "warning do not use while driving or operating machinery, works fast!' I decided to put the headphones to her ears. Inside of five minutes her eyes popped open and she looked side to side. I jumped up and said, "Oh my God! A Miracle."

When my sister came in, I was so excited to share the news. I asked her to play it on her shift. My whole family started playing it on their shift. We started seeing her become more alert and moving more every day. The nurses were amazed at witnessing A Miracle. My mother graduated from hospice four months later. To God be the Glory!

In 2022, six and a half years later, my mother no longer has a feeding tube for meals and eats three meals a day plus snacks, she watches television and has her favorite shows. Although she is still nonverbal, she communicates with her eyes, head, smile, laughs, and high-fives. We take her out in her wheelchair every Friday–Sunday for a ride and dinner.

My mother may not talk or walk but she is still here with us, bringing joy to our lives. Thank You, God! A Miracle!

Writing this book has become so special to me because my mother always said she was going to write a book about my paternal grandfather. He was a person that always lived below his means. He used to have a money room—a place where he threw money inside a room. I remember as a kid, I would follow him to it, and there was money everywhere, coins and dollar bills. Although this book is not about my grandfather, he, too, was a believer, and read his Bible daily and stood on God's Promises.

THE 72-HOUR MIRACLE

One Monday morning, I knew I needed to find some properties for an investor, and I was looking at everything. While looking, I noticed a new listing of a property that would have been perfect for different investor. My phone died which resulting in me not being able to follow-up immediately. However, I remembered to call him back about 9:45 p.m. I checked to see what was the latest time this investor had called before and when I realized he had called me as late as 10:15 p.m., I decided to call him. I told him about the property. He inquired about another property I had showed him two weeks prior and decided to make an offer. I left the agent a message and she contacted me the next morning. The seller was not saying yes or no, but we should put the offer in writing. I contacted my investor, and he met me at my office. We wrote the offer to close in seventy-two hours if we received an acceptance in two hours. The title company needed to know by 3:00 p.m. that day to make it a possibility. Time was of the essence in order for us to make it happen. The agent said it would take the attorney longer than that to prepare the deed. I received verbal acceptance a half an hour before the deadline. I received the contract at 3:30 p.m. I immediately sent the contract to the buyer and title company. The title company said to check on Thursday to see if we were closing Friday. I called Thursday afternoon, and no title work was in. The agent said to check back in the morning since she would know by Friday morning. I did my usual routine and read the *Upper Room* and the *Daily Bread* with corresponding scriptures. I read the Prayer of Jabez then I wrote my gratitude—one of the things I was grateful for was closing that day. I went about my business, then I received a call from the title company asking me if I would like to have a closing today? I said, "Praise, God"! I shared with her what I had written that morning she replied, "It must be in the stars and the moon lining up."

I said, "No. It was God! God made it happen! A Miracle"!

MIRACLES HAPPEN EVERY DAY, EVERYWHERE, TO EVERYONE

The Raid

In the early 1980s, I used to hang out at a popular nightclub called Foxstrap. I was friends with one of the bartenders. One night she got off work early and wanted to go to her friend's boyfriend's apartment right up the street. I agreed. Before I got in her girlfriend's car, I remembered I had a bag of weed on me. Something told me to take just a little bit, so I did. Then we went to her boyfriend's apartment. When we arrived at the apartment complex she pointed at his apartment. I saw a white man, although mixed couples were uncommon at the time, I said to myself, 'Okay, she has a white boyfriend.' I told them to go ahead, and I would catch up. I had an uneasy feeling, but I said, okay. I watched them enter the apartment, but I decided to keep walking past the apartment and bid them good night. As I walked past the apartment, someone came from behind me, interlock my arms, said, "Ma'am you are under arrest," and walked me into the apartment. When I walked in, more than ten people were being detained. The police officer asked for my ID. I gave him my college ID, he proceeded to search my purse; he found my weed. I was so nervous I almost peed on myself. Thoughts were running through my head: 'What will my parents say…Am I going to jail?' Then the police officer told me because of the amount on me I would not have to go to jail. However, he was giving me a summons. Thank God I didn't go to jail. A Miracle.

My friend's girlfriend drove us back to the club. They went back in, and I went to my friend, Marian Foxworth's (RIP) house where I found refuge. She consoled me and told me everything would be fine; she would even go to court with me. I was also blessed with a friend that had a lawyer on retainer that he referred me to. I picked Marian up and headed to court. We said a prayer before going in the courtroom that I would be fine. When the judge called my case, I was praying, 'Lord, please don't let me go to jail." The judge heard the case and acknowledged that the policeman 'carried me into the apartment', and that was a violation. Just like that, my case was dismissed with no court costs. The judge said, "Ma'am you are free to go." All I could do was thank God. A Miracle. I never found out whose apartment I was in or who the boyfriend was. God gave me mercy and my parents never found out (until this writing).

Mark 11:22-24

And Jesus answering saith unto them, Have faith in God. For verily I say unto you, That whosoever shall say unto this mountain, Be thou removed, and be thou cast into the sea; and shall not doubt in his heart, but shall believe that those things which he saith shall come to pass; he shall have whosoever he saith. Therefore I say unto you, What things soever ye desire, when you pray, believe that ye receive them, and ye shall have them. Amen.

Psalms 23

The LORD is my shepherd; I shall not want. He maketh me to lie down in green pastures; he leadeth me beside still waters. He restoreth my soul; he leadeth me in the paths of righteousness for his name's sake. Yea, though I walk through the valley of the shadow of death, I will fear no evil: for thy art with me; thou rod and thy staff they comfort me. Thou preparest a table before me in the presence of mine enemies; thou anointest my head with oil; my cup runneth over. Surely goodness and mercy shall follow me all the days of my life; and I will dwell in the house of the LORD forever.

Prayer is your connector to God. Just say His name.

I challenge everyone reading this book to start journaling your miracles for thirty days and see how truly blessed you are.

Herman's Story

Herman shared his story about working in a meat packing company, they were really busy. He was on a scaffold sealing the meat, when an uncertified coworker was driving the forklift and hit the corner of the scaffold. Herman fell eighteen feet. He remembered the fall, but nothing afterward, he woke up in the hospital not able to move anything. Herman went through therapy with a chiropractor and was walking sideways for about eight months. Then, something happened, and he was put back in the same position as he started. To see him today, you know it was God's Grace that healed him; he doesn't look like he was ever injured. He is walking upright with no limp. Look at God! A Miracle.

Philex's Story

I met Philex at a sales meeting. He was the highlight of our motivational segment. He shared his story about how he was injured at a construction site. Through frustration with his coworker, he stomped his foot, and a sheetrock nail went through his foot to the bone. He cleaned it with peroxide and thought it would heal. Later that week he noticed it was oozing and not healing. He went to the doctor and found the nail in his foot and an infection. After six months, it was still not healing and gangrene had set in. The doctor had to remove the top half of his foot. The next six months it still had not healed. The doctor said the infection was spreading. Philex looked down his leg and saw a band around his thigh just above his knee. He showed the doctor where he saw the band, the doctor didn't see anything. He asked Philex to use his pen and draw where the band was. When the doctor did an x-ray, that was exactly where they needed to remove his leg. Thanks to God, he showed him "where". A Miracle.

Philex is now out of his wheelchair and using a walker with his prosthesis. He is also learning to walk on crutches and he will eventually be using a cane. Thank God, A Miracle!

Chad's Story

When I first met Phyllis Willoughby, I knew she was special. You see, I instantly knew that she had some of the same experiences with God in her life as I have had. It is very hard to explain how I knew this, I just did.

Let me first take you back about fifteen years. I was a bar owner, and was very successful, and very naughty as well. The party life never ended, and the cash just flowed right with it. Finally, after five years of this, I felt a supernatural tug at me I could not explain. I fought it by drinking more and partying more (if that was possible). It only got worse. I knew I was doing the wrong things in life and there had to be more. As a child I was raised in church every Sunday and most Wednesday nights. I was rebelling against that, too.

The realization that God is inside all of us and wants to have a relationship with us hit so hard that I had to change my life completely. Trust me, it is not an instant process and one which will go on forever as we all try to do the right thing in our daily lives. There was only one perfect man. Once I realized that I did not have to be perfect to have God in my life, the pressure, burden, and guilt was demolished. I planted myself back into church and started praying and reading my Bible some. God loves us so much; I actually feel those words come to life, as they are living right now in my life.

About ten years have gone by since I started turning my life around and putting God first. When you do that, you start to notice miracles, that God works for you every day. Some are so *minute*, and some are tremendous, but I am now realizing God's Handprint in all aspects of my life.

So here I am five years ago making money with my real estate investment business and helping clients through online lead generation. I was the top producer in my company for years 2008, 2009, 2010, and 2011. Throughout this time, I achieved my real estate broker license without knowing why I wanted it. I just happened to be an Associate broker. Looking back, I can see God's Plan in my life without me knowing it. So, guess what happened next? I was making lots of money, and here comes God again, calling me and pulling at me. To do what, I asked? To open my own real estate firm, not for myself but for agents to learn what I have so I can be a blessing in their lives. Trust me, I did not want to do this. I didn't want the overhead of the firm, the agents pulling at me, and I didn't want anything getting in the way of the fun I was having. The realization that there was more to life than just me having a good time was hard to swallow. There was another realization that God was putting into me;

seeing others change their lives with my blessings was going to be more fun than anything I had ever done!!

Even after knowing all of this, I still pushed off the calling to open this real estate firm for four years. Finally, I gave up and said, "Okay, God. I'm doing it, and it is in Your hands. I have no idea how I'm going to make this work and get agents, and I have no idea how I'm going to pay for the lead generation platform for any agents that I do get. That is all I know, so every little detail has to come from you, God."

That's when the daily miracles started happening right in front of me. First, the online lead generation platform that normally has a two-year waiting list was thrust into my lap with a start date exactly where it needed to be. I just had to find a building to rent. The perfect office was available right across the street from my closing attorney and business partner. I explored many other offices for rent around town, but none were suitable. I spoke with the landlord, and to my amazement, he had turned down many willing tenants for the office space. He really liked me and cut the rent almost in half, throwing in two months free for me to get started. Can you see God's Hand in this yet? Next, I reunited with a friend of mine that happened to be another broker. She and I started dating and we both said we would not mix our businesses into our relationship. That was not God's Plan either. He pulled us both together to make this happen. She has been the biggest blessing in my life and business, and I could not see how this would have worked without us together. The next miracle came when I needed someone to be the office manager. I had no idea where to find one or how to pay one. Glenda, my girlfriend, knew Cheryle, a 27-year-old office manager for the biggest real estate firm in Tidewater. She was available and agreed to come work for us. Best of all, she could be flexible in her schedule. These are miracles right from God lining up front of me. The power and grace of all of this is so overwhelming that I can't it put into words. Since we opened, agents have flurried in, and we are growing. The money to pay the bills is there, too. It is truly all in God's Hands. Success or failure, I know that I am on God's Winning Side, and that He has a plan for me, and will never let me down. Even when things may look like a failure, just around the corner, BAM!! VICTORY IN JESUS!

An Anonymous Story

An attorney shared his story with me. He was walking, headed to the courthouse one morning. As he was walking, every ten steps he had to stop and put his briefcase down to catch his breath. He finally made it to the court to handle his case. The judge asked him if he was okay to handle the case. He told the judge he was. The judge then told him that he needed to immediately go to the hospital. It was a blessing that he listened to the judge. He went to the hospital, and they discovered he had three blood clots in his lungs. A Miracle.

The Miracle Wedding

Our wedding day had arrived! I met my high school sweetheart in 1974. We had lost track of each other for almost thirty years. After reuniting through Facebook, a courtship that connected Virginia Beach to Orlando, the "Big Day" was finally here.

Whoa! Before I am found guilty of the longest run on sentence in the history in the English language, perhaps a little back story is in order. Let's fire up the Caterpillar and dig right in!

We had met her senior year in high school. We dated all through college; separate schools in Nassau County, Long Island. We had landed decent jobs and decided it was time to get engaged. Well, the best intentions don't always go the way we expect them to. The engagement ended. Life relocated me to Virginia; she went into the military and was stationed in Germany. All communication ceased.

Fast forward to 2010, I'm perusing Facebook one evening, and upon doing an intensive search, not dissimilar to the scene in *Sleepless in Seattle*, I locate my lost love. She now had a different last name, but the pictures she had posted were unmistakable. Holy cow! I must have revisited that page ten times before I got up the nerve to send a friend request.

After what seemed like the longest week on the Gregorian calendar, she had accepted.

Does anyone need a Kleenex at this point?

We had resolved to Facebook messaging and texting for the better part of six months; thinking that would be playing it safe. Then one night in June, at around 9:15 p.m., I get a text: *"I'm just sitting here watching a movie....why don't you call?"* I was just sitting around watching a movie, leading the life of a stereotypical, swinging middle-aged bachelor. I called!

We spoke until 3 o'clock in the morning! Twenty-seven years had passed. It might as well have been twenty-seven minutes: same voice, same mannerisms, same laugh.

I had been taking care of an aging family member who had had some recent surgery and was responsible with setting up some senior care and other custodial duties. After several months of back and forth between work and two living situations, I had finally gotten back to my normal routine.

I was exhausted, and you could hear it in my voice. My sweetheart called one evening and said that I probably could use some time off. Agreeing to what seemed a like generic observation, (something about Mars vs Venus here) she proceeded to invite me to Orlando for a visit! I accepted. What does someone say when see a former fiancé after a lifetime? She pulled up to the passenger pickup area of MCO in a Sebring convertible with the top down on a warm summer's night, "What's new?"

After a brief period of awkwardness that didn't even last to the toll plaza, it was 1975 all over again, save the disco music and the platforms.

After a great visit, then another, then her visiting me up north, both of us began to wonder if God, The Universe, Life had given us a second chance We both concurred in the affirmative!

Fast forward to November 2013, the wedding is all planned. It is to take place on the balcony of one of the most graceful ladies to ever bless the sands of St Pete's Beach—The Don Cesar Hotel. It would be facing the Gulf of Mexico at sunset, harpist, formal attire, all systems go. Everything was planned to the nines, with the exception of the torrential downpour that had continued without ceasing throughout the day. Logistically, you pass through a large reception room to access the balcony, so that in the event of inclement weather, you simply back up twenty feet and you're back indoors. Harlequin-ally????? it was a tremendous disappointment.

The wedding was set for 4:00 p.m. At 2:00 p.m., the rain stopped, and our wedding planner called, and the room was in a mild state of hyperventilation. "We have a break in the weather she gasps! If you want, we can go ahead with the outside ceremony!" I agreed. As fate would have it, our room had a downward, unobstructed view of the balcony. There are no words to describe what I was about to witness over the next thirty minutes. Courtney and her worker bees drying off tables and chairs, hanging bunting, setting flowers, doing a day's prep; faster than the rain we just had! 'My kingdom for a video camera,' I thought. Nobody is ever going to believe this!

The ceremony begins with a harp, sunset, and a vision of loveliness that I had only contemplated with my mind's eye. The perfect wedding did exist, for us and our thirty guests. It concluded with hugs and kisses, lots of color photographs, and well wishes. As the guests proceeded downstairs to our reception room, I was the last one to exit the balcony. I looked over my shoulder as I stepped back inside to give Him a wink and a smile. The rain immediately returned. Coincidence?

Our wedding Miracle!

Another Story

I was blessed with reading a story about a young solider that was humiliated about his belief in God. The captain thought he would humiliate the young soldier in front of the whole troop and asked him to drive a jeep and park it. The solider replied he could not drive. Captain said, "Let your God help you." So, the solider prayed and got in the jeep and drove it perfectly and parked it. He turned around and asked why was everyone crying? The Captain went to the jeep, opened the hood. There was no engine. Everyone said, "I want to serve your God!" The God of impossibilities as possible. A Miracle. (Unknown author)

The Motorcycle Gang

I was living in Key West, Florida in 1982. My friend, Lucy invited me to help her drive to Fort Lauderdale to a concert. We gassed up and we were on our way. We got about sixty minutes out before the car broke down. It was about 9 p.m. and everything was closed, including the only gas station. We were surrounded by mangroves (thick jungles). We could hear all the animals. We were in complete darkness and I couldn't even see my hand in front of me. I had a Bic lighter. I flicked the Bic, just to get a glimpse of light, until we walked about a mile back to the gas station to use the phone. When we finally got there, we flagged a state policeman down, and told him our situation, and to please send other cars to check on us. The state policeman left. We knew that anyone we called would take at least an hour and a half to get to us. The whole time I was being eaten alive by huge mosquitoes. Then suddenly, a biker gang appeared. They started circling us and revving their bikes, popping wheelies and yelling out obscenities. It was in this moment I dropped to my knees on hard concrete and started praying to God and thanking him for protecting me, this black girl with her white friend in the early 1980s with this all-white motorcycle gang. Then suddenly, I heard the gang start peeling off one-by-one. It was clear, a Miracle happened that night.

Short Miracle Story 1

I just happened to call my sister setting up a luncheon appointment with a colleague when she decided to invite me to a Christian Networking event. What a blessing! First, I was available to attend, and at the event, the speaker was Judge Robert McDonnell. We received "a message"! He told us three things to help our business:

1. Do what you say when you say.
2. Operate with Integrity.
3. Vision - look at the orchard.

He also told us that if we have made a mistake, repent then keep going. After the event, I introduced myself to him. He told me I was anointed to do great things for God and the world. I then shared I was writing a book on miracles. He grabbed my hand and proceeded to pray. While praying I could feel the intense energies running up and down my body. He said a powerful prayer and concluded with a prayer for wisdom. God will give me the words to share with the world.

Short Miracle Story 2

Mr. John P. Yancey was about 12 years old, and he needed braces. The dentist told his mother he needed one of his wisdom teeth extracted. As you can imagine for a boy that age it was like getting brain surgery. He was totally stunned when the dentist said that on top of the fear factor. Ten days praying, he was riveted with fear. As the extraction day was approaching one of the Catholic nuns went to get him on the playground and that he looked very upset. He told her what was about to transpire that afternoon. She told him to go down to Chapel which, he did, and came back before recess was over. He went to the nun, and she gave him a piece of caramel candy which he started chewing, and low and behold the tooth came out! After school he told his mom, and she said maybe it's the wrong tooth. They went to the dentist, and he confirmed that it was the right tooth. A Miracle.

Client's Challenge

I remember a text from my client that said, *"Bless the name of Jesus. Tell three people that you love them, and hug them, and bless one of them with $5."* Well, I missed the *"one of them"*, I thought I had to give $5 to all three. When I received this text, I was at a gas station. My first thought was 'I don't have it to give.' I was putting $40 in my gas tank. My next thought was to just put $20 in the tank, and then I got change for the other $20. I turned around in the store and walked up to a young lady (a complete stranger) and said, "Hello, I just want to tell you I love you and give you a hug." I hugged her and put $5 in her hand and said, "This is a gift from God." She was so surprised. Then I went to put gas in my truck. I had to find two more people to bless. I spotted another lady pumping gas so I walked up to her and did the same thing. She was quite amazed. I said, "I have to find one more before I go back to the office." That's when this lady pulled up. When she got out of her SUV, I greeted her with a smile and said, "I just want to tell you I love you and give you a hug." I gave her a big hug and she responded, "I needed that hug." Then I blessed her with $5. It felt so good to give someone what they needed without being asked. I thought my mission was complete as I headed back to the office. I got to the office and something was tugging at me to keep going to the 7-11 store. As I looked around, I saw another lady pumping gas and I did the same thing again. She shared she was really having a bad day and this way a blessing.

I left feeling on top of the world because I had done God's Work and put smiles on people's faces. I quickly realized it was not about me, it was about God letting them know he was there for them. Later, I texted my client back, *"Done."* It felt so good to bless one more than asked. I spoke to my client the next day and shared what I had done. The following day he blessed me with a tank of gas plus $500. I had no clue blessings were around the corner. The moral of the story "Give and it will be given unto you." Don't block your blessings.

The Firewalk

It was on a Saturday afternoon, we all gathered at Unity Church. We spent hours preparing for the Firewalk through different strengthening exercises, group exercises, and meditations. I still did not know if I was really ready for this challenge. Now it has become a faith walk for me. Sixty-five of us lined up for the challenge. As I looked at those hot, burning coals, I asked myself, 'Am I crazy for doing this?' However, I knew I had to do it to get over any fears. When it was my turn, I looked at that long line of hot coals, the crowd was cheering me on so I stepped out on faith and kept my eyes on God. I walked the hot coals all the way to the end where the coach hosed down my feet and we celebrated. People ask me how could you have done that? My response was, "Only with God." I kept my eyes on him and completed the Firewalk without any burns on my feet.

A Miracle!

What it symbolizes to me, we go through trials and tribulations but when you focus on God, you get to the other side, and you celebrate. Just remember, no matter how bleak it looks there is another side.

How do I feel God's Energy? I focus on him through prayer, mediations, or by reading scriptures. I get this overwhelming energy running through my veins. There is power in His

Name. The power of God's Energy is powerful: flowing thoughts, flowing energy.

Just know that God is with you even when you don't think you feel His Energy, it's there. It is so powerful. It's like a confirmation of whatever you are doing is right with God. Just know, God does speak to us, however, we all have to be quiet and listen to hear His Voice and feel His Energy.

Grow with God and heal. God's Energy is powerful, yet calming; like fuel that drives the engine. Praise Him, praise Him, that's what God wants. He wants to be your everything…your healer, your way-maker, your friend, your rock. God is always with you! Talk to Him like a friend but know He keeps your secrets. Remember He sees all and knows all. Man can say, "No," and God says, "Yes." A Miracle.

Trust, trust, trust.
God wants you to believe in Him. Life is a faith walk, when you walk in faith, countless blessings (miracles) will happen. Just believe God has no limits.

The average Firewalk is six to twelve feet. Ours was fourteen feet.

MIRACLES WE TAKE FOR GRANTED

When you wake up in the morning you open your eyes, and you can see. A Miracle. You are breathing, you can get out of bed, and walk. A Miracle. You can think rational thoughts, you can speak, you can go to the bathroom, you can flush. Turn on the lights, the light comes on. Go to the refrigerator, there is food. Do you have a roof over your head, air conditioning in the summer, and heat in the winter? God is all around us and in us; let God's Light center you, touch one person at a time and be a living witness.

I challenge everyone that reads this book to start journaling your miracles for thirty days and see how truly blessed you are. Prayer is your connector to God, just say His name. God gives us inner guidance to listen, to listen and to follow, when we follow, blessings flow, and little miracles happen. Gratitude is the key. When you are in a grateful state, Miracles continue to happen like an unexpected check that comes in the mail.

God has all power. I am not belittling miracles, but I am showing you that you are surrounded by miracles every day, every month, every year. You just need to recognize what they are and be grateful. By being grateful in every situation, the door opens for more miracles.

GOD'S MESSAGE TO THE WORLD

Believe in Me. Blessings will flow. Receive your daily miracles, share your miracles; be A Miracle and watch the world be a better place.

I am the source of all sources. I am the Way-maker.

"Don't be afraid to ask Me anything. Nothing is too big or small for Me. I just want to be a part of your daily lives." Sometimes we have not, because we do not ask. Faith must come afterward. "I am working in the background to provide your request, however, you must not doubt."

All God wants us to have a relationship with Him. And when you have a relationship with God in your actions, choices, speech, and your life, God is love. When you go to God, He is there for you always, healer, confidant, provider and way-maker.

When you doubt, you cancel the order.

Miracles are big and small and happen daily. Miracles are unexpected blessings that let you know God has intervened.

Sometimes that missed turn was *A Miracle*, you were not involved in that five-car pileup—*A Miracle*.

I just want you to understand that we all receive miracles in our daily lives. "Just acknowledge Me and all your blessings."

It is about understanding God and all that he does for you. "All I ask, is to acknowledge Me for all my acts."

God is a global guide. He hears and sees all everywhere, just listen and hear God's Voice because He is speaking to us, we just have to listen. We are living miracles. No man can cause or create a Miracle, it is always God. He is with you always. You can always talk to Him and feel Him, if needed.

Glenda's Miracles

Where do I start? Which story shall I choose? Our very lives are miracles. The planet is a miracle. The very fact we are living on this planet is a miracle. Because of the "bad" in my life I can appreciate all that is 'GOOD", in every little detail, every "coincidence", and every experience.

It is a miracle I can see the good still in people, places, and things after all I have experienced by people. But I do!

I was born and raised in a very small town. My mother left my father when I was one year old. Till this day, 40 years later, I have never met him. They were poor, not even running water in the home. My mom remarried, let's say, a middle-class man from our area, and life was good until they divorced when I was nine years old.

My mother was now divorced and working in ship building for minimum wage and raising three children alone. In a small town, being a bastard, dirt poor, and no man in the house, you quickly become a social outcast. Times were different then and there in that area of North Carolina. We were not a normal/average family at that time or place.

The friends we had were told by their parents they could no longer be our friends, nor talk or play with us. The parents acted as if they never knew any of us. Our stepfather's family disowned us all.

But luckily with God I knew there was a better life for me and I did not have to believe we were somehow "less than" because of our family status, new income level, or because society now called us names. I was still the same person. Nothing in me had changed. Even at nine years old I knew they were the ones that were wrong.

After years of this treatment and watching our small family of four struggling to survive and fit in the best we could, at 15 years old, I became pregnant. With a weak moment of shame and knowing they would ridicule me further, I dropped out of school with only a 9th grade education in order to avoid the public shame.

At 16 years old, I had a beautiful baby girl, born out of wed lock. I named her with her fathers last name to avoid the thought of her being called a bastard, however when asked to wed by her father I said no. I knew I did not want to spend the rest of my life with this man and could not lie at the alter. I was willing to hear their remarks and whispers versus lie to God and myself with those vows.

Talk about a Social outcast, oh my! I was a baby having babies, a high school dropout, trailer trash, bastard child; feeling life my life was ruined and I would never amount to anything.....and the list goes on.

But the Miracle here is GRACE. With God always in my ear and my heart, from a small child on, telling me others were all wrong and not to listen.

A few short months later my daughter's father for the first time in our relationship pushed me down and threatened me, while holding our daughter.

I witnessed my mother being physically abused, strangled, shot at, and we (her three children) were told once while he was beating her, that we were going to watch our mother die. So needless to say, I knew where this could lead and that was not the life I wanted for my daughter and me. The next morning, I called my aunt to come pick me up, I packed what I could, and she picked me up. I left the state.

I had moved out of my mother's home when I told her I was pregnant (a year earlier) because I knew it was not safe for me there. I had not seen her for months and had no idea where she lived other than a state away and the name of the city. At this point I was still 16 years old and my daughter was 6 months old. We drove to her city, found a phone booth, looked up her name and I saw her number and her address. I called her and said I need a couch to sleep on. She allowed me to sleep in her living room. **Strength, Courage and Faith, A Miracle from God at only 16.** To move to an unknown city with no know-how and just know I will make it here, for my daughter, somehow. All with no Fear, just persistence.

I used my brother's bike until I could get my own. I hit the local mall and applied everywhere! God said, "You do not know any of these people and none of them know you. None of them know your past, here you can start over and be yourself." So, I Did. By the time I was 17 years old, I obtained my high school GED and became a manager. By 18 years old, I was the General Manager of a large retail chain, supervising people from 18-80 years old.

By 21 years old, I purchased my first home and a brand new car in the same month, all on my own.

By 25 years old, I was married.

By 28 years old, I was a Realtor, making more money than anyone I knew. By 34 years old, my daughter graduated high school and started college.

By 40 years old, I had two grandchildren, my daughter graduated with a bachelor's in fine arts. My husband of seventeen years walked out on us and moved out of state. Time for more strength, courage and faith, and for God to deliver me more miracles...

He did. Months after my husband left, I meet a man, left my current real estate firm of thirteen years, and we started a real estate firm together within weeks of us dating. Now, months later, our firm is growing by leaps and bounds and our agents are changing their lives through this firm. Others in our industry cannot believe our progress and success in such short time and the power couple we became.

What will the future hold? I don't know. But when every day you keep faith, courage, and believe in yourself knowing God is there for you, because when you look back at your life and see you beat the odds that were stacked against you and you realize that you could not have done it alone. You'll have no doubt, this world is full of miracles and the story of your life will only keep

BELIEVE IN getting better.

MIRACLES!

By: *Glenda C. Powell-Johnson*

I ASKED FOR A LITTLE BIRD

March 1, 2015 at 9:00 in the morning changed my life forever when I received a knock at my door. The knock on the door was so loud and threating is still bothers me when people knock. It was Homeland security, Us Marshall and News reporters. I was placed under arrest and snatched away from everything I loved and worked for. I was being detained for some charges that I got in trouble for twenty-five years ago. I turned my life around completely since then. I was born in hackney England April 21, 1970 and we came to America at the age of ten. I Lived in the United State all of my life and have not been back to England since I left.

I walked Out of my home in Portsmouth VA in Handcuffs and I died at that moment. The pain in my chest and spirit was too much for me to handle, but I never lost my Faith. I was scared and frightened. All I could hear was my dog barking as they Ice agents closed my front door. I was at my lowest point in life and the feeling was unbearable, confusion plagued my mind and feeling of hopelessness was sinking deep into my soul.

My life was heading in the right direction, so I thought, I graduated from medical school, and I was working for the number one Pediatric Doctors in the tidewater area. My life as comedian was taking off; amongst everything else I was doing. I attended church and was very active in the community. This knock on the door took me deep into my past life. God was closing a chapter in my life and opening a new one. I didn't know what God was doing and I didn't understand. The minute I was put into their transportation I started praying and I asked God to forgive me for being so scared, forgive me for the wrong I had done. I didn't know where I was heading or what to do. All I could do is put my faith in God. I cried and I asked God to give me peace and let me know everything would be alright. I wanted this

pain in my heart to go away and stop hurting me. I kept praying the whole time I was in the car and asked a lot of questions to the arresting officer. He had no answers and was very vague. It was just another day in the office for him and the changing of my whole life for me. It was a nightmare and it took me to the lowest point of life. My parents would be devastated, my family and friends, my dog, my job I worked for four years and my company. I was placed in the back of a truck with another detainee and his handcuffs were so tight around his wrist that his hands were bright red and he was in a lot of pain. He didn't speak English very well. I prayed for the both of us; I asked God to keep us safe and we needed Him. My handcuffs were tight and cutting off the circulation in my hands. With much suffering joy would soon come, I didn't see it and I didn't understand why this was happening to me, why I was being punished, why my life was being turned upside down? Lost and confused, I was being sent into the wilderness; alone and so afraid. The cold of winter set deep inside my bones and I was losing my faith as we drove off to the headquarter. I prayed so hard and out loud, I asked the officer to loosen my handcuffs because they were too tight, yet he wouldn't listen. As we drove off the misery only set in deeper and my world got a lot darker. I didn't know what I was praying for and couldn't believe this was happening. My vision was blurry from the tears in my eyes. During the journey I commented several times about the handcuffs being too tight all which were ignored. We were delayed and stopped by a cargo train and we sat still for about 15 minutes and that is when it happened. I called upon God to remove these handcuffs and the stop this pain. God was listening I asked the officer to loosen the handcuffs, in the name of Jesus and he listened, he took the first detainee out the truck and placed his handcuffs in the front and loosened them, placing him back in the truck. Then it was my turn - same process.

I was taken out of the truck, my handcuffs removed, placed in the front and ankle cuffs put on. I look up in the sky and asked God "Lord I do not know what is going on, but I am scared, Lord, help me please, I trust in You. Show me a sign that everything will be ok, show me a bird a little bird. Show me something." Right at that point, on the pole across the street a Redtail Hawk took flight in all of its beauty. I never in my life saw anything more beautiful than that, the peaceful feeling it gave me, had no comparison to anything in my life.

The love and protection of God was upon my soul. The guidance and grace of God surrounded me and embraced me. It was brief but it will last a lifetime. For the first time in my life, I felt safe and protected. All I could say was, "Thank you Lord for answering me when I called upon You." My pain and suffering would soon pass. This magnificent creature was so powerful and symbolic for life and living. God's timing was *so* perfect even in the midst of my storms he provided me with a sign of faith, a promise that He had me then, He has me now and forever. That was my sign from God that everything would be okay. I was detained for three months and released. I was able to retain my job, house, family and my dog. It was a faithful journey and I found faith in a Redtail hawk. The hawk that I named 1221 followed me throughout my whole incarceration. Every time I went outside or looked at television, the 1221 was there. God sent me the biggest sign and all I asked for was a little bird. To God be the Glory!

Darren Kerr

MORE MIRACLES

Glenda's Story

I had this dream. One of those dreams that stick with you and touches you at your core.

I was a man on a beach, possibly an island, with two other men. All of a sudden, the crashing wave caps turn into a large heard of wooly mammoth type animals with long brown hair and huge white tusk. They stormed the beach as if off to battle and being directed to do so.

The next set of waves crash with the caps turning into hundreds of grey horses with a silver pattern of a square spiral all over them, like a tiger has stripes this was their fur pattern. They were strong, fierce and mighty, yet stunningly beautiful. One came over to me, looked at me with his large brown glass like eyes and telepathically said, "Remember this symbol". I rubbed him on his nose and he headed on as back to the mission of war. The next wave came in with tribes people who were running off to war. I looked at my friends and said the time has come. And we ran back to our huts. I told my wife "This is what we have prepared for, get ready"

And then I awoke.

The dream was so clear, so vivid in color, It stayed with me and reminded me often to find that symbol. So I began my search for this symbol for weeks with no luck. A few weeks later I am out with my daughter, her boyfriend, and my husband at the time. We talked about going yard sale shopping for years but never did. So this morning we all happened to have no plans and all decided to go.

We made a wrong turn looking for an address, got lost, and ended up at a flea market. So we said perfect! We will do that. Our first stop once we parked was a Rastafarian man and his wife and child with a tent in the parking lot with tables of books and some jewelry to raise money for charity for children in Africa. What kind of book does he have........ Books on ancient symbols!

I tell him about the dream and draw him the symbol. Right away he wants to know my birth name and my heritage. Then he proceeds to give an explanation of the symbol. I buy a few books and we go into the building to shop around.

While shopping, I keep hearing a voice say go outside he has something to tell you. It keeps on and gets stronger and more persistent. So, I tell the family I have to go outside and they decide to come with me, even though we had not been in long nor had we seen even half of the shops. As I walk out he is putting the last book in his car. I wave at him and he says come here I have something to tell you. He shrugs his head to say step away from the others. My daughter and her boyfriend walk away but my husband decides to stay with me. The man says: "God wants me to tell you something. He is working things out." Then bends down to act as if he is trying his shoe… which had no strings. Looks up at me and then nods towards and looks at my husband and says "there is something in your life that does not belong there, don't worry God is taking care of it. Do you understand me?" I said, "Yes and thank you". I immediately got chills all over my body. At this time I was very unhappy in my marriage, but believed no matter what you stay. Marriage is forever. Good or Bad. And I was searching for answers. I could not believe the feeling of relief from this message.

A week later my husband was offered a job in another state. The job offer was less money and the cost of living was higher where he wanted to go. With me having an all commission job it made no sense to me to lose my income and move for less money and higher cost of living. This made no financial since. I told him he could go but I would stay here. I thought this is it!!! But then they did away with the position in his company so he did not go. Well, a year and half later he was offered another job out of state. He did not tell me about it nor ask me to go. He came home and told me I want a divorce. That he needed to find himself and be alone. A week later I find out from my daughter that he had applied for the job and was moving 1500 miles away in two months.

My daughter had just moved back home with a 1-year old and another baby on the way. She had left her boyfriend. She had been home two weeks when he dropped the bomb of needing to be alone.

Thankfully this happened when it did and not a year and half before. I had learned a great lesson in love and about myself. I could love again even after all he had done. I had put my ring back on and was ready to forgive the affair, porn addiction, financial misuse and all. It had been about two months of us working on things and all seemed perfect. Then he dropped that bomb.

Good news also was that all three of the cars were just paid off, my income had lowered over those two years of trying to work on the marriage, but I had somehow managed to pay off all of my debt. So now he was the bread winner and was taking care of me for a change. He also walked out and completely abandoned us. Two years earlier when I was wanting to leave I would of paid him alimony, I would have been left with debt, but instead he gave me the house, pays me alimony, and agreed to stay on the mortgage for fifteen years so I do not have to refinance it.

All in Gods timing. Just breathe, put it all in God's hands and watch the miracles take place.

The message God gave through that man that day was a constant reminder for me and helped me weather the pain of divorce. Just remember if you be still, and wait, God will answer and he can do things in ways you could of never imagined possible.

Glenda C. Powell

Leila's Testimony

My name is Leila and I want to share my testimony of how I received miraculous healing and deliverance through the power of God. Nothing shows God's amazing love and power like a miracle. The power of God is present to heal you. I am here today to tell you my testimony that God has touched me. In Mark 5:19 Jesus told those He healed to tell others "what great things the Lord has done for you." Doing so brings healing in your own soul, and it brings honor to God's Kingdom on earth.

I know in my body and in my soul that God has stepped in and showed me His Divine power and brought healing upon me. My pain is gone, and I recovered when the doctors didn't think I would. In 2015 God healed me from a subarachnoid hemorrhage which is bleeding in the space between the brain and tissue covering the brain. A subarachnoid Hemorrhage is a serious condition which can lead to an aneurysm, brain damage or death.

The night before I ended up in the intensive care unit of the hospital God was clearly speaking to my mind and heart through His word. He spoke to me and said that this sickness is not unto death but for me to see His power in my life. It brought to remembrance John 11:4, "This sickness is not unto death, but for the glory of God, that the Son of God may be glorified through it."

Prior to finding out that I was bleeding from my brain I had been experiencing severe headaches and blurred vision for over a week. I thought they were symptoms from the cold that I had. The next day after God was speaking to me I went to work with an excruciating headache to the point where I ran to the ladies room holding my head and crying out for help. God is so wonderful! He had orchestrated that day for everyone to be in the right place at the right time on my behalf. Someone touched me and said what's wrong! I looked up and it was Ruth, a good friend of mine that lives in another town. I asked her if she could take me home and in comes my supervisor saying no l am sending someone to take you to the emergency room.

While at the emergency room I explained to the doctor my symptoms and told him that the pain in my head felt like I had been shot. He left the room suddenly and came back and said they were going to run some tests and could I call someone to come and be with me. I thought that was strange because all I had was just a cold. I looked down at my phone because I received a text message from my daughter asking me what I was doing and I told her that I was at the emergency room because I didn't feel good. She said she was on her way to be with me and I thought that was strange too because she was at work and all I had was a cold. I never asked her to come and be with me. God had my day all planned out.

After the test results were in, the doctor advised me that they would have to transport me by an ambulance to the hospital because I was bleeding from my brain. I started shaking and was very scared until my daughter reminded me who I was in Christ. I thought about the scriptures that came to life in my spirit the night before and understood what God was revealing to me. God would not allow fear to come upon me, he kept me calm and at peace during my entire stay in the hospital.

I was admitted to the intensive care unit at the local hospital under the care of three neurologists. The physicians explained to me and my family the severity of my condition and if I had to have brain surgery that there could be a possibility that I could die during the procedure. God assured me that I would live and that He would be with me every step of the way. The neurologist tried to promote fear and did not understand how I was able to sit up and laugh with them and my family when I could die any moment. I told them that I was not going to die and I was not going to have to have surgery that God was going to heal me.

The next day the neurologist scheduled me for an angiogram where they go into a vessel to take images of your brain to see the location of the bleeding. When the neurologist came to my room with the test results he said *you* were correct. The bleeding has stopped and we do not have to perform surgery. I would like for you to stay in the hospital for a week for observation.

I stayed in the hospital for seven days and had seven nurses from seven different countries. On the day I was to leave the hospital one of the neurologists came to visit me and he said

I saw you reading the Bible and pouring into others and I want you to know that I am a believer too. He said "you are a miracle!"

God heals because He has compassion and mercy for us. God heals for His glory and in response to faith. The Bible is full of miracles that speak of a living God. He is the God that makes the impossible possible. He makes all things work together for good and He wants to bless you.

I humbly relay this testimony to you and declare that in this situation it was God's will to manifest His power on that day at that moment for His glory.

Leila Holt

Leslie's Story

When I got married to my wonderful Jack back in 1998, I was 32 years old and he was 55 years old. We both knew what that meant, as time progressed, we would age, and he would probably go first, but we didn't care. We knew God gave us each other and decided to go for it!!!!

After our first year of marriage, Jack developed severe pains in his side, so we went to the old Bayside Hospital......they gave him a nuclear scan and there it was....a mass in his liver. We sat on the hospital bed together and decided ok Lord, it was better to have one year with each other, than none at all so we rejoiced in what we had together, prayed, cried and waited for the news.....

There was a lady I worked with that had a prison ministry, where she wrote and kept up with 400 inmates.....I shared what was happening with me and Jack and she prayed with me then put the word out to hundreds of her Christian inmates in prisons all over the country. They picked one day and they all prayed and fasted for Jack even though they did not know him....

He finally had his liver biopsy and the doctor who did it, said Mr. Wills, good news, this is puss. We were stunned, the doctor was stunned??? I knew, Jack knew, and the doctor knew it was cancer, but when the biopsy was done, it turned out to be a liver abscess???? There was a mass that was like an orange that was separated with little chambers that just had puss from an infection THAT WAS TREATABLE.....three months of antibiotics every four hours thru a port and a trip to MCV in Richmond, but still that was nothing compared to what it could have been.

My best friends dad had just been diagnosed with a liver mass and he was dead in three months....here is the miracle......I know, that I know, that I know, and Jack too, had cancer BUT because hundreds of inmates turned their food away for a day and prayed on his behalf, GOD SHOWED MERCY and changed it to something else. The bible tells us that Jesus first miracle, turning water into wine at the wedding was NOT supposed to be his first miracle, but because He had compassion for his friends, He did it anyway. No one can tell me otherwise, Jesus had compassion on Jack and gave him something else, because God honored all those inmates' prayers and supplication on behalf of Jack!!! God is truly faithful, day, after day, after day, Amen...

Leslie Wills

DARE TO BELIEVE

As you come to the end of this book, I invite you to reflect on the Miracles in your own life. Perhaps you have experienced a miraculous healing, a chance moment of divine guidance that led you to where you are today. Whatever your story may be, know that it is a testament to the power of God, Beliefs, Faith, and Hope.

May this book inspire you to see the world through eyes that make you look for the miracles that surround you every day, and to believe in the possibility of the impossible. Remember that miracles are not just grand events that happen once in a while, but they can be small moments that add up to a life filled with wonder and grace, they are the hand that reaches out to help us when we fall, the kind words that heal our wounded heart and courage that ignites our spirit to overcome fears. Miracles are around us, waiting for us to see, embrace and share.

So, DARE TO BELIEVE, in the miracles of your life, and let them be a source of strength, comfort, and joy. May they remind you that you are not alone, that you are loved beyond measure, and that you are part of a greater story that is unfolding. May your heart be filled with gratitude for the miracles that have touched your life and may continue to be a beacon of light and hope for others. Thank you for sharing in this journey of miracles with me.

May you always remember to DARE TO BELIEVE!

30 DAYS OF JOURNALING

Phyllis Willoughby

Write about a small act of kindness that someone did for you today.

Write about the time when you felt truly grateful today.

Write about a moment today when you felt empowered or inspired.

Write about a moment when you felt truly loved or appreciated.

Did you receive any expected help or support today? How did it make you feel?

Write about a moment today when you fell into with your intuition.

Write about a moment today, when you felt truly connected to your spiritual self.

Write about a moment today where you felt truly free.

Write about a moment today when you felt truly blessed.

Write about a moment today when you felt truly connected to your purpose for calling.

What was something you notice today that you usually take for granted?

Write about a moment when you felt completely in the flow.

Write about a moment today when you felt completely safe and secure.

Write about a moment today when you felt completely grateful for life and the people in it.

Did you witness a transformation or breakthrough today in yourself or someone else? What was it?

Did something happen today that made you feel inspired to take action or make a change? What was it?

Did you experience a moment of clarity or insight today? What did it reveal?

Did you witness an act of forgiveness or compassion today? How did it make you feel?

Did something happen to you today that you were described as miraculous. What was it?

What was the most amazing thing that happened to you today and why?

Write about a moment today you felt truly at peace.

Write about a moment you felt truly authentic.

Did you experience a moment of transformation or growth today? What did He teach you?

Did you witness a healing or recovery today? How did it make you feel?

Did something happen today that you weren't expecting or surprised you? How did it make you feel?

Did you experience a synchronistic event, coincidence, or serendipity today? What happened?

What is something you felt today that you have been avoiding or denying?

Write about a moment today when you felt truly connected to your inner wisdom.

What did you notice today that gave you a sense of wonder or awe?

Phyllis Willoughby

ABOUT THE AUTHOR

I became a licensed Realtor in 1986 only by the Grace of God! I had dropped out of college (Old Dominion University and Norfolk State University) with only 18 hours of school requirements to graduate. I had completed all my major (Marketing) and minor (Economics) requirements. Due to running out of money I pursued becoming a flight attendant because I love to travel and love people. I was on Piedmont Airlines wait-list and I worked as a hostess for Fun Tours bus lines. As time passed, I grew more and more depressed with the frustration of not finishing school, not working as a flight attendant and finding a professional full time job. I had been in bed for days then one night I decided I would just end it all. However, I knew committing suicide was a sin, so I was led to read some Bible scriptures and ask God for forgiveness. Then I was led to pray a prayer of humility; I proceeded to tell God all that I wanted in a job so I asked him to lead me, guide me, and I would follow. Then God showed me real estate...I said to myself "I have no interest in real estate and I don't know much about it, only a house is a house and a townhome was just that, a town-home. God reminded me of my prayer and I said, "Okay, God I will follow". God saved my life that night! A Miracle.

I made a commitment to apply myself, study and not partying until all work and assignments were completed. I said to myself, whenever I get the money to go to school and I would make this commitment. Low and behold the following week I had a day trip to Atlantic City with Fun Tours, that's where God sent one of his angels to give me the money for real estate school. It happened so fast, I wasn't sure if I was ready to make the commitment but I heard God's Voice saying "you asked me to lead and guide you and you would follow." Now that I have provided the money, I could not get to the real estate school fast enough to register for class. Well, I made the commitment and passed the PSI on the first try. To God be the Glory! I knew then it was my mission from God to help educate first time buyers and investors build wealth. Providing service beyond their expectations. Real Estate became my ministry instead of a career. I am always praying for or with my clients for guidance and favor. God led me to business to help people realize their dreams. I have enjoyed this opportunity for 36 years servicing the community's needs. It has truly been a faith-walk....I would take that walk all over again!

Phyllis Willoughby

Allison Nausam Trav Dir. of Sr
301 7360240
Tomeka (Allison) Ass
Social Srv Designee
- Sytina Smith   Exec Director
(301) 736-0240 EXT 113
sytsmith@chs-corp.com

Corporate Offc   Ohio
Communicare Company
(614) 443-7210

CARE Plan MEETING?
Sr Dir Dwerj@Futurecare.com   Jody? Dir
GravesM@FutureCare.com   Sr Exec Dir
Clinical Admiss Dir
Brenda   Ethics & Compliance Hotline
         Navex Global
Home Line
Line   sytsmith@chs-corp.com